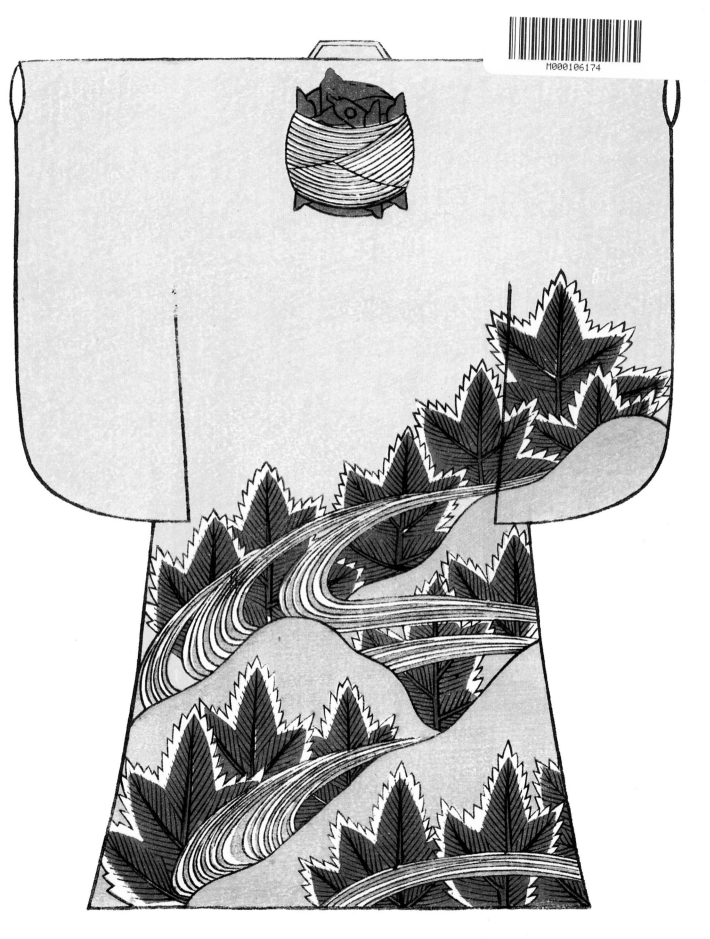

PLATE 1

PLATE 2

JAPANESE WOODBLOCK
KIMONO DESIGNS
IN FULL COLOR

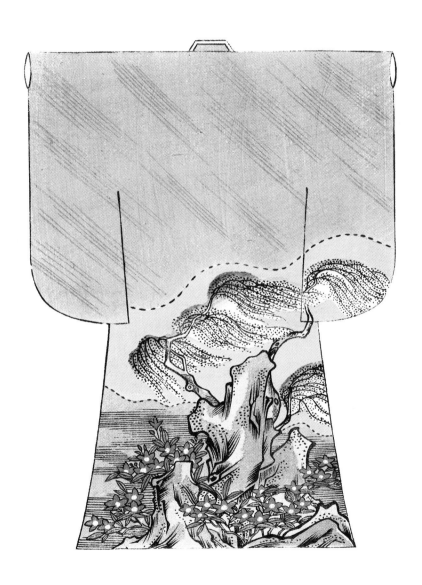

DOVER PUBLICATIONS, INC.
Mineola, New York

NOTE

Among the most recognizable garments in the world, the Japanese kimono (the word means "clothing") has inspired the decorative genius of Japanese artists for centuries. Thanks to the popularity of *ukiyo-e* (images of the floating world) woodblock prints in the West at the beginning of the twentieth century, the kimono-clad maiden became one of the quintessential images of Japan. Although the prints in this volume are hard to date, they were likely produced in the late nineteenth century, in the heart of the Meji era. Reprinted here in beautiful full color, the kimono designs include traditional Japanese nature imagery: irises, bamboo, cranes, flowers, stylized birds, dragons, waves and other motifs. Subtle, delicate, and refined, these designs reflect the high degree of inspiration and craftsmanship characteristic of the Japanese woodblock print.

Bibliographical Note

This Dover edition, first published in 2007, is an unabridged republication of a rare, undated, late nineteenth-century Japanese volume.

DOVER *Pictorial Archive* SERIES

This book belongs to the Dover Pictorial Archive Series. You may use the designs and illustrations for graphics and crafts applications, free and without special permission, provided that you include no more than four in the same publication or project. (For permission for additional use, please write to Permissions Department, Dover Publications, Inc., 31 East 2nd Street, Mineola, N.Y. 11501.)

However, republication or reproduction of any illustration by any other graphic service, whether it be in a book or in any other design resource, is strictly prohibited.

Library of Congress Cataloging-in-Publication Data

Japanese Woodblock Kimono Designs In Full Color / Dover ed.
    p. cm. (Dover Pictorial Archive Series)
Republication of a late nineteenth century Japanese volume.
Includes bibliographical references and index.
ISBN 0-486-45602-1 (pbk.)
    1. Kimonos—Pictorial works 2. Wood-engraving, Japanese—Themes, motives.
I. Dover Publications, Inc.

NK4784.A1J27 2007
746.9'20952—dc22

Manufactured in the United States of America
Dover Publications, Inc., 31 East 2nd Street, Mineola, N.Y. 11501

PLATE 3

PLATE 4

PLATE 5

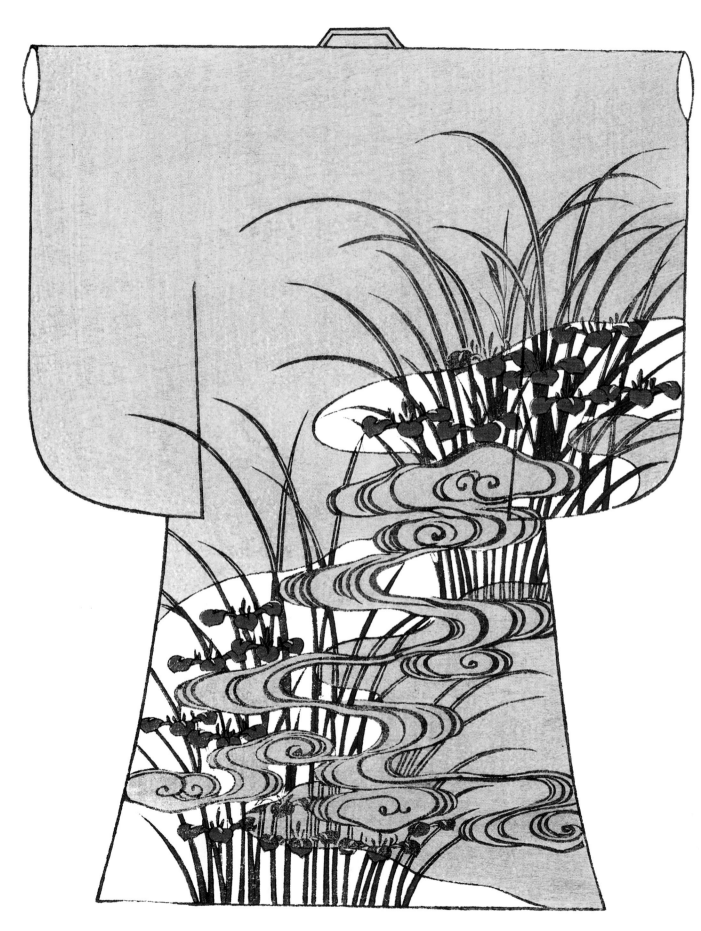

PLATE 6

PLATE 7

PLATE 8

PLATE 9

PLATE 10

PLATE II

PLATE 12

PLATE 13

PLATE 14

PLATE 15

PLATE 16

PLATE 17

PLATE 18

PLATE 19

PLATE 20

PLATE 21

PLATE 22

PLATE 23

PLATE 24

PLATE 25

PLATE 26

PLATE 27

PLATE 28

PLATE 29

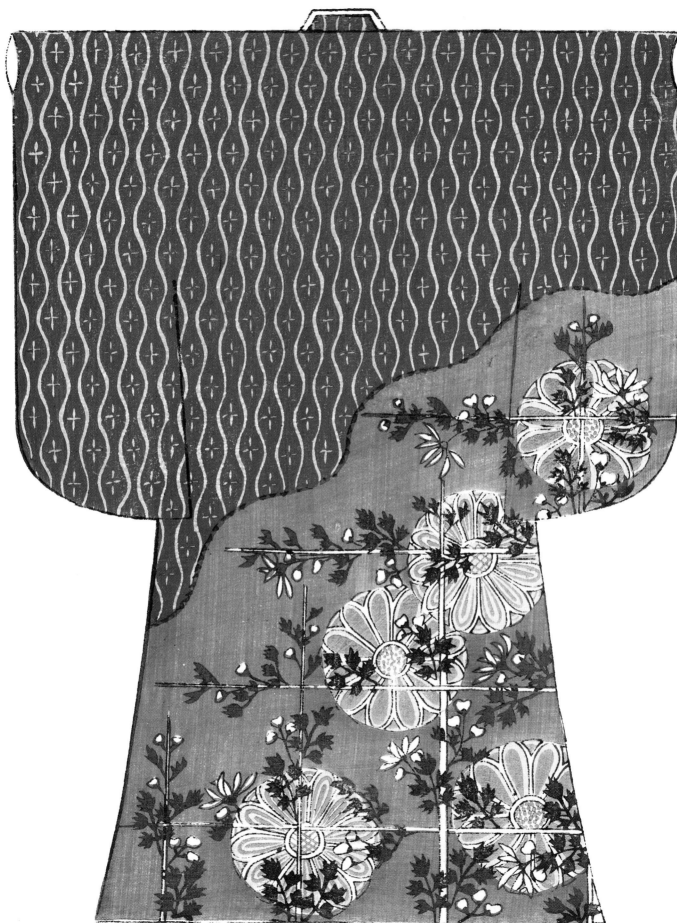

PLATE 30

PLATE 31

PLATE 32

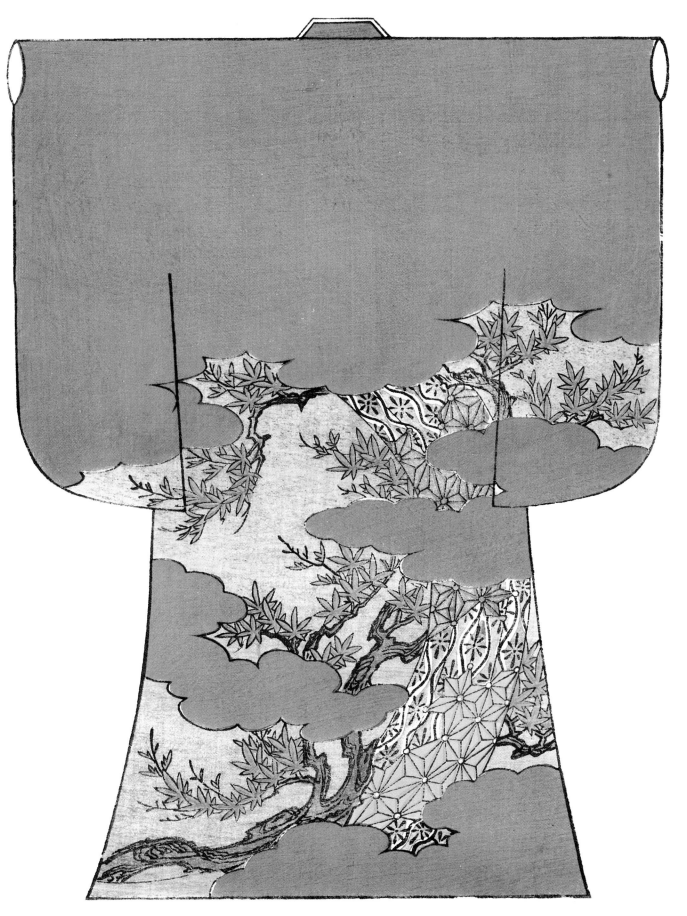

PLATE 33

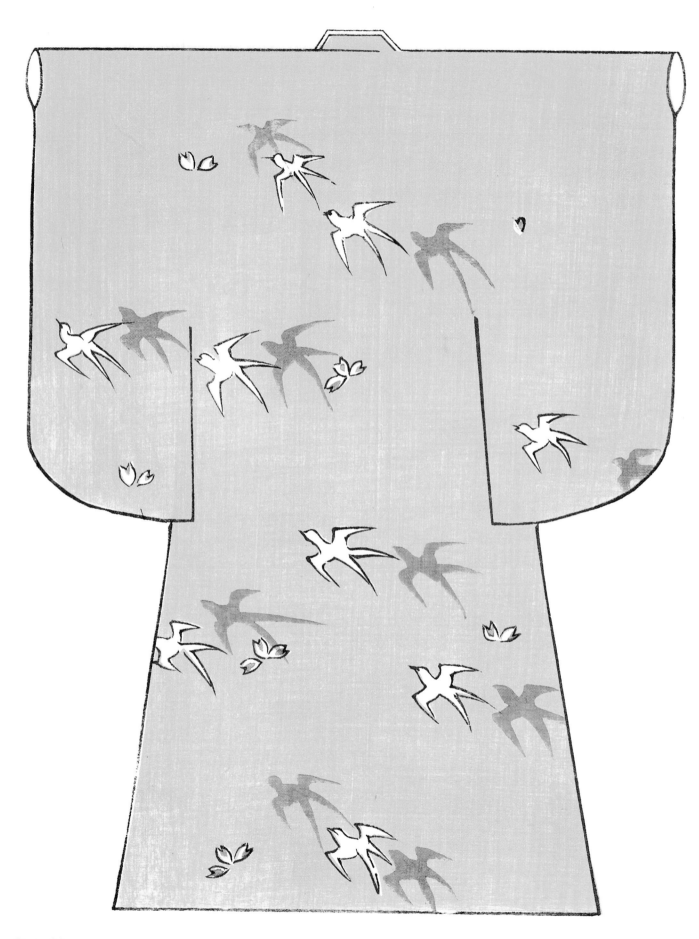

PLATE 34

PLATE 35

PLATE 36

PLATE 37

PLATE 38

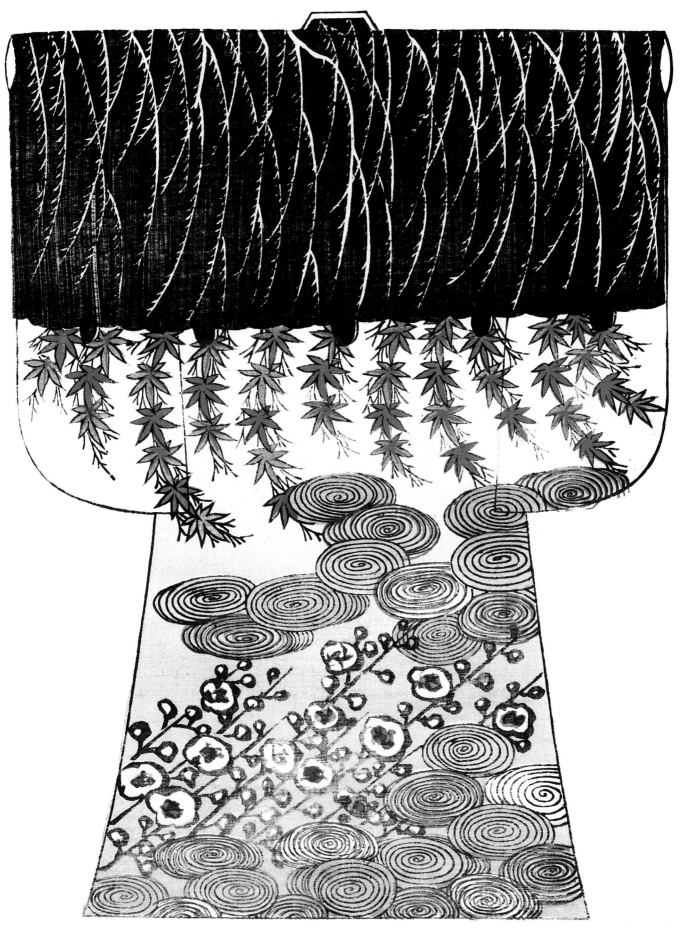

PLATE 39

PLATE 40

PLATE 41

PLATE 42

PLATE 43

PLATE 44

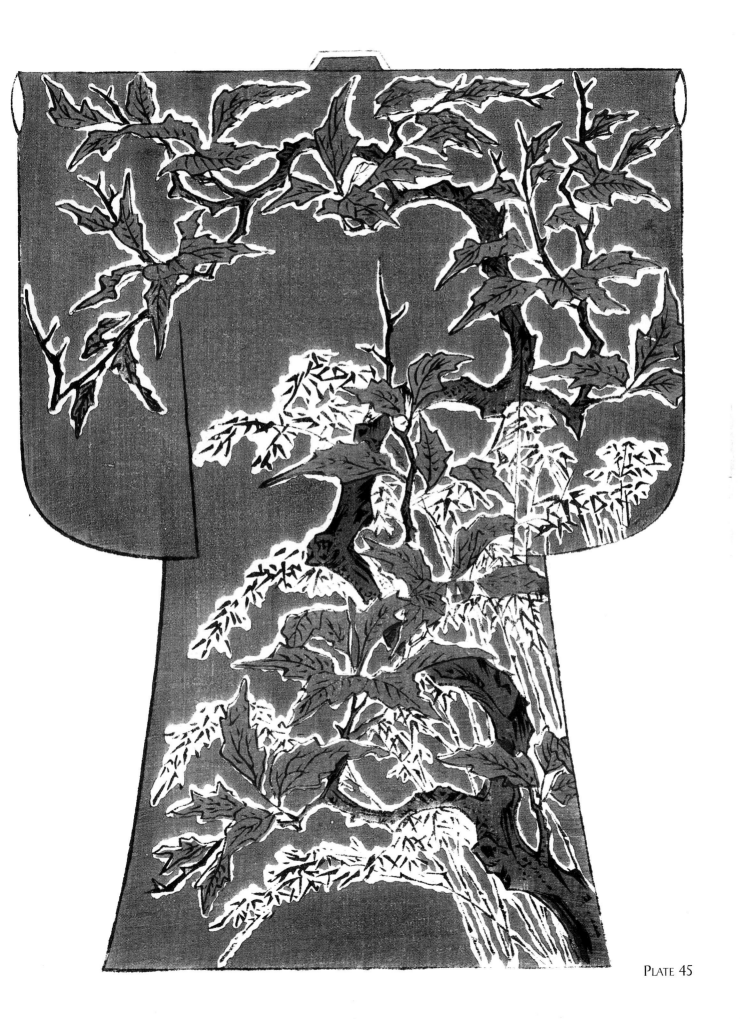

PLATE 45

PLATE 46

PLATE 47

PLATE 48

PLATE 49

PLATE 50

PLATE 51

PLATE 52

PLATE 53

PLATE 54

PLATE 55

PLATE 56

PLATE 57

PLATE 58

PLATE 59

PLATE 60

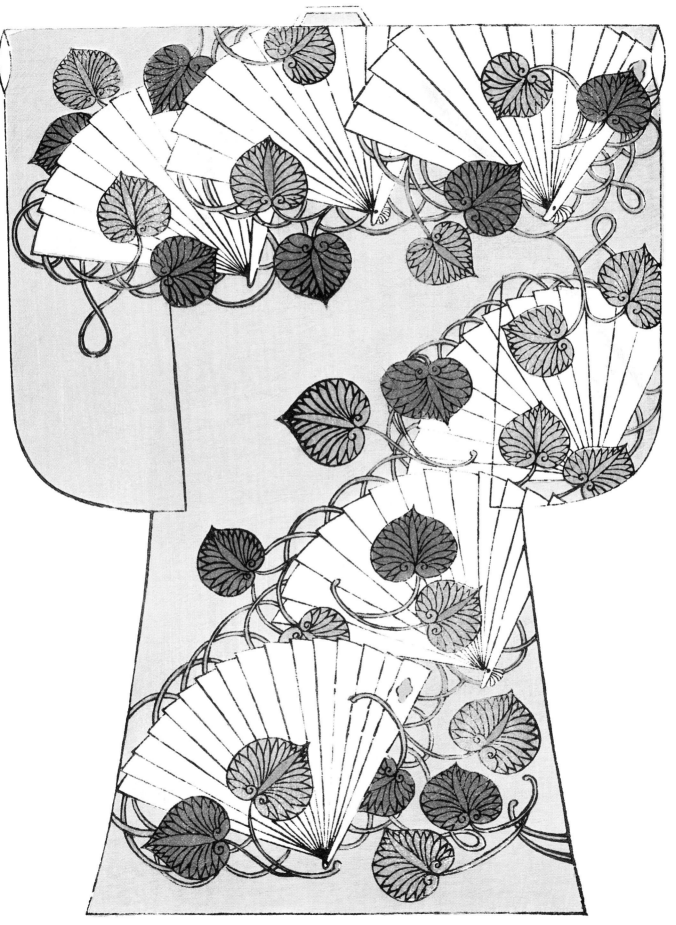

PLATE 61

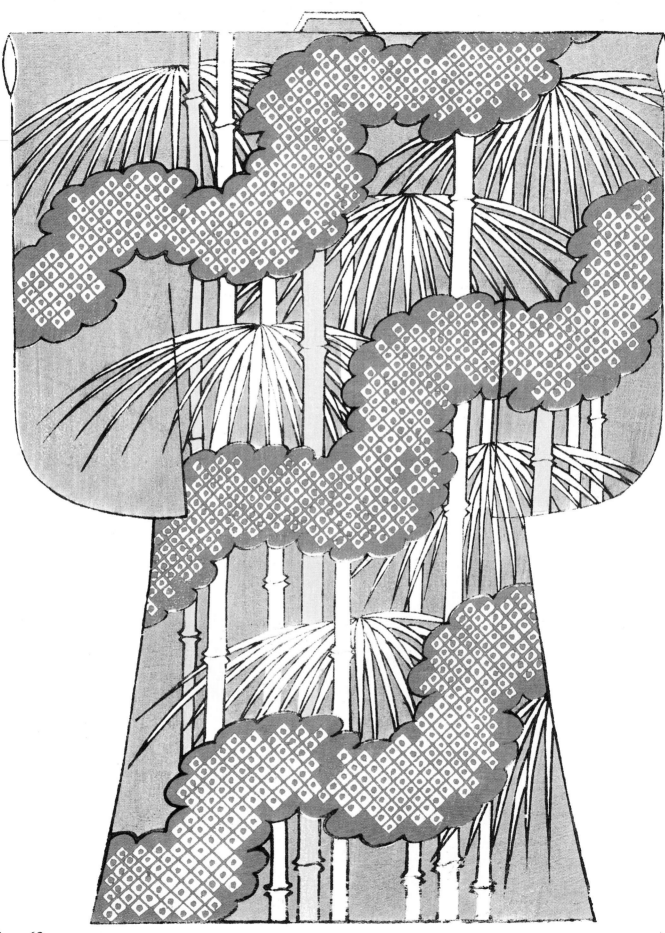

PLATE 62